PEGASUS ENCYCLOPEDIA LIBRARY

3D
FISH

Managing editor: Tapasi De
Designed by: Vijesh Chahal, Anil Kumar
Illustrated by: Suman S. Roy, Tanoy Choudhury
Colouring done by: Vinay Kumar, Sonu, Kiran Kumari & Pradeep Kumar

CONTENTS

What are fish? 3

Characteristics of fish 5

Adaptations 10

Types of fish 15

What do fish eat? 19

Habitat 20

Relationship with humans 22

Some interesting sea fish 23

Test Your Memory 31

Index 32

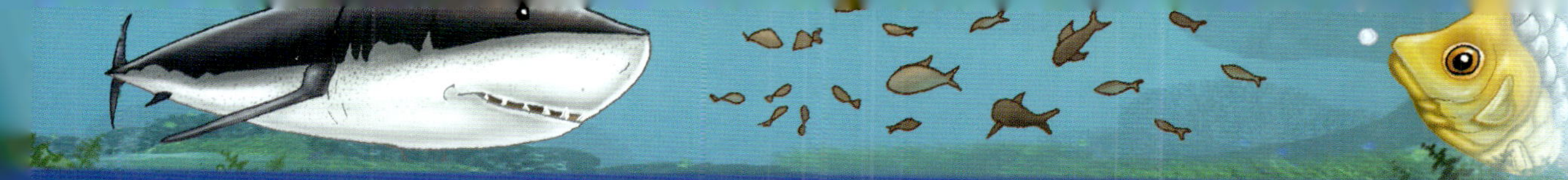

What are fish?

A **fish** is any gill-bearing vertebrate that lives in water and has a skeleton made of either bone or cartilage. Most fish are cold-blooded which means their body temperatures vary according to the surrounding temperature. Their internal body temperature is therefore the same as the surrounding water.

Fish are abundantly found in most bodies of water. They can be found in nearly all water environments including streams and lakes located on high mountains to the deepest parts of the oceans.

FISH

There are more species of fish than all the species of amphibians, reptiles, birds and mammals combined. There are about 25, 000 known species of fish. More are being discovered everyday. Some scientists think that this number might reach up to 40, 000!

Fish breathe through **gills**. Gills perform the gas exchange between the water and fish's blood. They allow the fish to breathe oxygen in the water.

Most fish swim using a **tail fin**. Muscles in the tail fin move it from side to side, forcing water backward and propelling the fish forward. Other fins help the fish to change their direction and to stop. The fins on their sides help them swim up and down. The fins on the top and bottom keep the fish upright. The **fins** on the underside help the fish to steer left and right.

The study of fishes is called ichthyology and scientists who study fishes are known as ichthyologists.

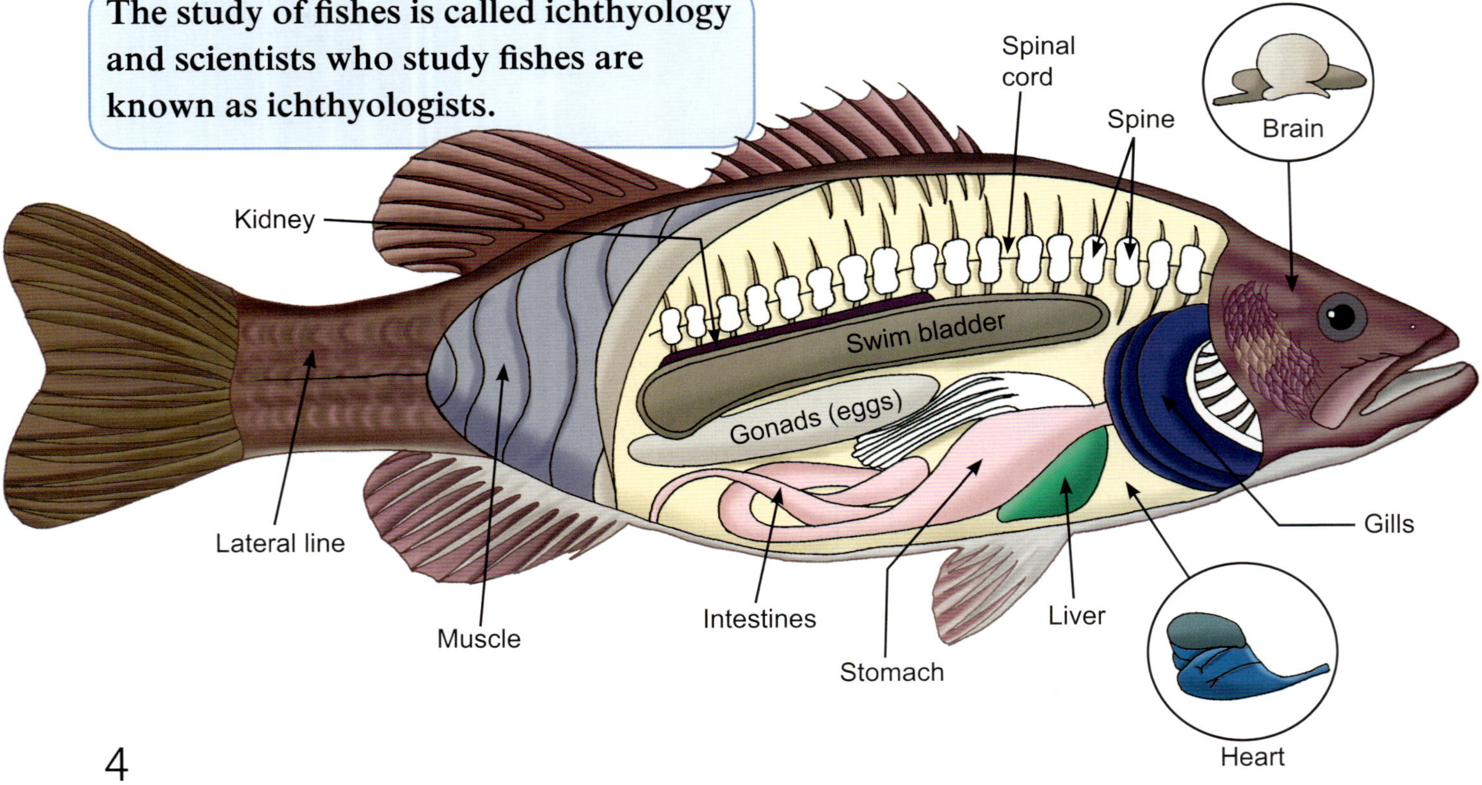

Characteristics of fish

Cat fish

protection against injury and infection. On the top of their scales, fish have a mucous covering. This mucus helps the fish fight bacteria. It also helps the fish to move through the water more easily.

Nature has made fish in such a manner that they are well-suited for living in water. The shape of their bodies, feeding habits and swimming behaviour are examples of the characteristics which is very typical to fishes only.

Skin

The skin of most fish is covered with scales. These scales are firmly attached to the skin. The scales offer

Scales on the skin of a fish

FISH

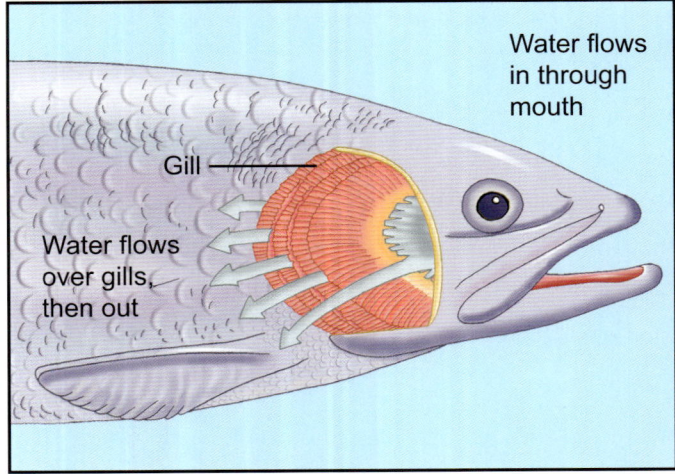
Gills

Respiration

Fishes do not have lungs like humans. Fishes breathe oxygen dissolved in water with the help of gills. Fish exchange gases by pulling oxygen-rich water through their mouths and pumping it over their gills. Some fish, like sharks and lampreys, possess multiple gill openings. However, most fish have a single gill opening on each side. This opening is hidden below a protective bony cover.

Body shape

The shape of a fish's body tells a lot about its lifestyle.

Astonishing fact

The lung fish can live out of water for as long as four years!

Most of the fish have a streamlined, body and are usually fast swimmers who are capable of great bursts of speed. A streamlined body is narrow at each end which makes swimming easier as they cut through the water while moving forward.

Characteristics of fish

Many tropical fish are flattened from the sides. Their body shape is very well adapted for hiding in the cracks and crevices of rocks and reef. They can move into these areas to escape their killers or to reach a food source that cannot be reached by other fish. Sometimes fish change colour also to protect themselves.

Some fish are flattened from top to bottom. Fish with such a body shape spend most of their time at the sea floor. Such fish can change colour too to match the colour of the sea floor.

Fins

Fins are used for swimming and sometimes for protection. The **pectoral** and **pelvic** fins are paired. The unpaired fins are the **dorsal**, **caudal** (tail) and **anal** fins.

Angel

Flying fish have wing-like pectoral fins that enable it to glide through the air!

FISH

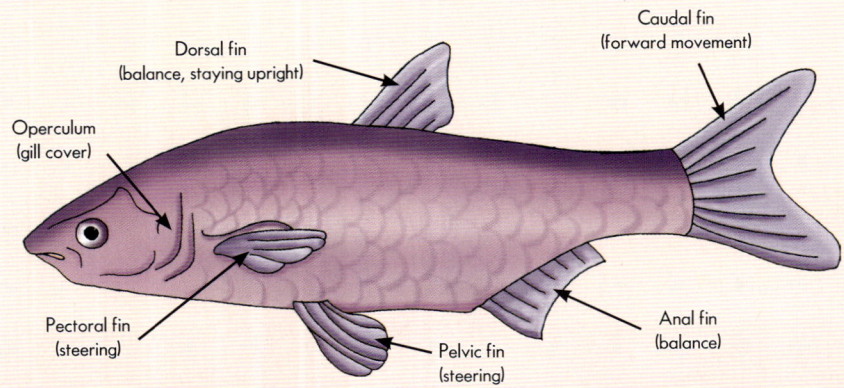

- **Caudal (or tail) fin**: This fin is responsible for pushing forward in most fishes.
- **Anal Fin**: The anal fin provides stability to the fish.

Tails

The shape of the tail can be an indicator of how fast a fish usually swims. Fish with crescent-shaped tails are fast swimmers and constantly on the move. Fish with forked tails are also fast swimmers, though they may not swim fast all of the time. Fish with a rounded or flattened tail are generally slow moving, but are capable of short, accurate bursts of speed.

The way the fins are used varies among different groups of fish. Most fish use their tails to move through the water and their other fins to steer with. The shape, location and size of a fish's fins are closely linked to its way of life.

- **Pectoral fins**: Pectoral fins are used for turning while swimming, although they can also be used for other functions such as tasting, touching, support and as a source of power for swimming.
- **Pelvic fins**: Pelvic fins add stability and are used for slowing down speed by some bony fishes.
- **Dorsal fin**: This can be a single fin or be separated into several fins. In most fishes, the dorsal fin is used for sudden direction changes and acts as a keel to keep the fish stable in the water.

Forked tail

Rounded tail

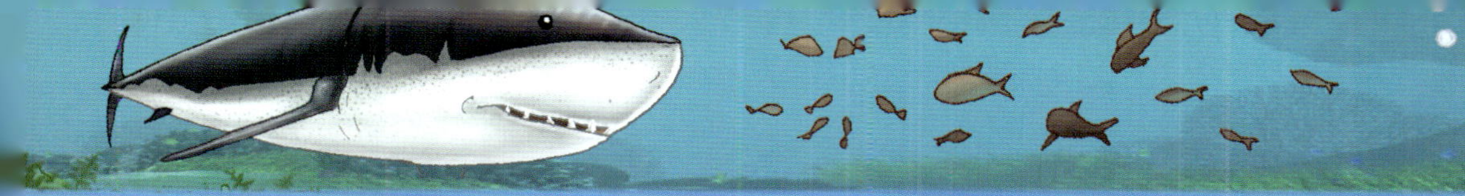

Characteristics of fish

Eyes

Many fishes have large eyes to help them see in the dark depths of the ocean when they go searching for food. Fish such as sharks have pupils that dilate (become wider) and constrict and some sharks also have an eyelid that closes from the bottom upward!

Reproduction

Reproduction in fish usually involves laying eggs that are externally fertilized, though a few give birth to live young. Eggs maybe dispersed into the water, laid in nests hollowed out in sea sediments, incubated in the mouth of the adult. There maybe no parental care or one or both parents may provide close attention during incubation, hatching and even the first few weeks of life.

> The Upsidedown catfish from Africa are famous for being the only fish species known to naturally swim, belly-up.

Adaptations

Fish have special adaptations which have helped them to survive in an environment completely different from that of humans. Some of the common adaptations are:

Swim bladder

The swim bladder is a unique organ found only in fish and is sometimes called the 'air bladder'. It is a smooth, gas-filled organ found in the abdomen of most fish. A fish will either increase or decrease the amount of air in the bladder to help it move up or down in the water. Without the air bladder, the fish would have to swim continuously to keep from sinking to the bottom. By adjusting the amount of air in the bladder, fish can adjust the depth at which they float.

Adaptations

Sight and sound

Most fishes have an excellent sense of sight and can see colours. They have ears but they do not have external openings. The ears pick up vibrations and help the fish in hearing and navigation.

Fish also have a unique navigational aid unlike anything found on mammals. The structure is called the lateral line and runs along the side of the fish. The lateral line contains small sensory hairs that can detect even tiny vibrations. This extra organ allows fish to navigate and hunt prey even in low light or cloudy water conditions.

Salt regulation

Maintaining the proper level of salt in the fish's body is critical to its proper health.

> Fishes were the first animals to evolve when life began on Earth millions of years ago.

Lateral line

11

FISH

Coloration

Fish display a wide variety of colours and colour patterns. Skin coloration can have many functions. Many fish have colour patterns that help them blend in with their environment. This may allow the fish to hide from a predator.

Fish coloration can also be useful in catching prey. Many sharks show coloration known as **counter shading**.

Sharks are dark on the dorsal (upper) side and light on the ventral (lower) side. So, any prey looking down on the shark will see a dark shark against a dark sea bottom, making it hard to detect the shark. Conversely, any prey looking up at the shark, will see the light belly of the shark on the light background of the ocean surface water lit by the sun or moon.

Climbing Perch Fish can come out of water in search of food and can also climb trees!

Adaptations

Young boxfish are shaped like a box!

the eyes so that other animals cannot tell where the fish is looking or even if it is a fish or not. Some fishes, like Butterfly fish have spots on their body that resembles eyes. This may serve to confuse their prey and their enemies alike.

Markings

Fish can also have disruptive markings to hide body parts. Species such as the Jackknife fish high-hat and some Angel fishes have dark lines that run through the eyes. These lines may serve to hide

Light organs

Some marine fish have the ability to produce light through **bioluminescence**. Most light producing fish live in mid-water or are bottom dwelling deep sea species.

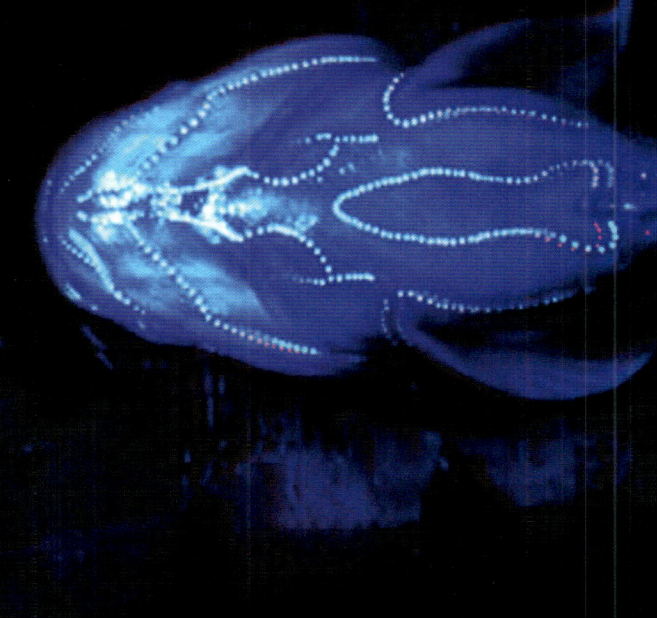

FISH

Toadfish

Electric eel

Venom

Many fish may use venom or poison as a form of defending themselves. Some examples of such fish are stingrays, chimaeras, scorpionfish, catfishes, toadfishes, rabbit fishes and stargazers.

> The Electric eel has an average discharge of 400 volts!

Electric organs

Fishes like sharks, skates and rays possess an electric sense system. Through this system these fishes are able to detect the weak electric fields produced by prey.

Some species of skates and rays also have electric current producing organs. With these organs, electric rays are able to shock their preys.

Types of fish

According to anatomical structure

Scientifically, modern fishes have been divided into three classes:

- **Agnatha**: The jawless fishes.
- **Chondrichthyes**: Jawed fishes that possess skeletons made of cartilage, and sharks, rays, skates and ratfishes.
- **Osteichthyes**: Jawed fishes that have skeletons made of bone.

Hagfish

Agnathan

Agnathan are also known as the jawless fish. They have no jaw, no scales, no paired fins and no bony skeleton. Their skin is smooth and soft to the touch and they are very flexible. There are two major types of Aganthan. They are **Hagfish** and **Lampreys**.

FISH

Chrondrichthyes

Chrondrichthyes fish have a cartilaginous skeleton; therefore they are also known as cartilaginous fish. Only the teeth of this species and rarely the vertebrae are made of calcium. Cartilaginous fish don't have swim bladders. There are over 980 species of cartilaginous fish. They include sharks, rays and chimaera.

Osteichthyes

Osteichthyes are also known as bony fish. Fishes that belong to this species are spindle shaped, oval and flattened. Skins are protected by protective scales. Another adaptation is **operculum**, a bone on the sides of the fish to protect the chambers that house the gills.

Rayfish

Shark

Chimaera

Types of fish

Bony fish are again classified into **ray finned** and **lobe finned** fish. Ray finned fish have thin, flexible skeleton rays. Lobe finned fish have muscular fins supported by bones.

According to the type of water

Another basis of division of types of fish is the type of water they inhabit. This division is primarily used for the purpose of keeping fishes in aquariums.

Tropical fish live in either salt or freshwater but need a warm (tropical) temperature to live.

> There are over 30000 known species of fish.

Coldwater fish too can live in either salt or fresh water but they need colder water temperatures.

Marine fish live in salty seawater. Usually marine fishes need tropical climate.

Freshwater fish live in freshwater and are usually found in inland rivers and streams of most continents.

17

FISH

Coelacanth

Fish that reproduce in fresh water and have offspring that migrate to the ocean where they spend their adult lives are called **anadromous** (e.g., Atlantic and Pacific salmon). In contrast, fish that reproduce in the ocean and whose young migrate to fresh water to grow into adulthood are known as **catadromous** (e.g., American and European eels).

According to their ability to tolerate saltiness in water

Fish are also categorized according to their **salinity tolerance**. Fish that can tolerate less saltiness of water (such freshwater fish as goldfish and such saltwater fish as tuna) are known as stenohaline species.

Flounder

What do fish eat?

There are thousands of species of fish living in oceans, rivers and other water bodies. It is difficult to classify the food which forms the diet of these fishes. Some eat other small fishes while other eat other sea creatures like algae, plankton, sponges, crustaceans, snails, sea urchins, worms and star fishes.

Habitat

Fish are found nearly everywhere where there is water with enough food, oxygen and protection. However, not all fish can live in the same kind of waters. Various factors are involved in the selection of a habitat for a particular kind of fish. Take a look at some of them.

Salinity

As discussed earlier, one major factor that separates fish is salt. Some fish cannot live in areas where there is much salt and others need salt in the water to live. However, some fish can live in both saltwater and freshwater.

Oxygen

Even though fish live in water, it needs an adequate supply of oxygen in the water. Living plants within a lake or

stream add oxygen to the water through photosynthesis— the process of using sunlight to make food. Oxygen can also enter water from the surrounding air.

Food

The amount and type of food available in water plays an important role in which fish will live. The amount of competition with other fish forms a factor also.

Habitat

Water temperature

Each fish has a different range of water temperature in which it can survive. Some fish can live in a wide range of temperatures, but some fish require particular water temperature to survive. Although fish cannot always find the exact temperature they prefer, they are usually found in water close to that temperature.

Water quality

Most fish are also sensitive to sediments, pesticides or any other pollutants in the water. Good-quality water will support more species of fish and greater populations of fish than polluted water. Stagnant, polluted or water lacking adequate oxygen will not support large numbers of fish.

Shelter

Fish need places to hide from its killers and competitors. They may also need places to rest if there is a strong current. Areas behind rocks, around sunken logs and branches, among patches of vegetation or in deep pools all provide fish with places to escape.

Migration routes

Most fish are very particular about where they will lay their eggs and raise their babies. They will only reproduce if they can find the right type of surface and the right water quality. Therefore fish often travel a great distance between where they live and eat and where they reproduce. Fish must be able to swim through all the areas in between if they are to be successful in their travels.

Astonishing fact

Desert Pupfish from south-western US and northern Mexico can live in hot springs which can have a temperature of 490° C!

Relationship with humans

Fish as food

Fish is a food of excellent nutritional value, providing high quality protein and a wide variety of vitamins and minerals. Fish, especially saltwater fish, is high in **omega 3** fatty acids, which are very important for a healthy heart and vital to normal brain development in unborn babies and infants. A regular intake of fish is always recommended by most nutritionists.

> Goldfish can outlive dogs and cats; they can live up over 20 years!

Fish keeping

Fish keeping is a popular hobby concerned with keeping fish in a home aquarium or garden pond. While most freshwater aquaria are community tanks containing a variety of compatible species, single-species breeding aquaria are also popular. Aquarists also regularly breed many types of cichlid, catfish, characin and killifish.

Many fish keepers create freshwater **aquascapes** where the focus is on aquatic plants as well as fish. Garden ponds are in some ways similar to freshwater aquaria, but are usually much larger and exposed to open weather.

Some interesting sea fish

Red Lionfish

Red lionfish is a venomous marine fish found around coral reefs and in the shallow waters of the Indian and western Pacific Oceans. It features a very bright red coloured body. It is as dangerous and predatory as a lion, which is how this fish got its name. One of its spines can cause painful puncture wounds immediately which may last for a week before fully healing. Lionfish grow to 30 cm in length and weigh up to 1 kg. It can move incredibly fast in order to catch its prey. It usually chases crabs, shrimp, molluscs and small fish.

Leafy Seadragon

The leafy seadragon is a marine fish and close cousin to the seahorse. It grows up to 45 cm. Leafy seadragons inhabit the shallow tropical and temperate waters of South and West Australia. The protrusions which cover the body resemble leaves and that's how it got its name. Leafy seadragons feed on plankton, algae and water dust.

Long-spined Porcupine fish

The members of the porcupinefish family have evolved an interesting means of defence. When threatened by a predator, they fill their bodies with water until they swell like a balloon. This makes them too large for the predator to swallow. Also they have pointy spines sticking straight out when it is inflated. If that's not enough of a defence, the porcupine fish's flesh is poisonous to most animals, including humans.

Stonefish

The Stonefish gets its name from its stone-like appearance. This excellent disguise allows it to blend in with the background as it waits for its prey to wander close enough to gobble. In addition to its gruesome looks, the stonefish has sharp, venomous spines that contain enough poison to kill a man!

Mushroom Scorpionfish

Scorpionfishes are characterized by their bizarre appearance and the numerous spines that cover their bodies. Similar to the lionfish, these spines contain venom strong enough to cause a very painful wound and even more serious injury to those who may have allergic reactions.

Deep Sea Angler fish

The deep sea angler is also known as 'common black devil'. The angler gets its name from the long, modified dorsal spine which is tipped with a light producing organ known as a **photophore**. Like many other deep-water fish, the angler uses this organ like a lure to attract its prey.

A strange fact about the deep sea angler is the fact that the male is smaller and different in appearance from the female. The male of the species is about the size of a finger and has small hook teeth, which it uses to attach itself to the female. Once attached, its blood vessels join with that of the female and it will spend the rest of its life joined to her like a parasite, getting all of its nourishment from her body. If the male is unable to attach to a female, it will eventually die of starvation.

Some interesting sea fish

Archerfishes

Archer fish are unique because of their peculiar way of hunting of insects and other small terrestrial animals from branches hanging above the water. It hunts by firing with great accuracy streams of water into the air to their prey, knocking down animals as big as small lizards or to the water's surface. Once fallen into the water, the fish dashes and gulps its prey. The fish can shoot up to 4 m.

Macropinna Microstoma

Macropinna microstoma is the species of fish belonging to Opisthoproctidae, the barreleye family. It is recognized for a highly unusual transparent, fluid-filled dome on its head, through which the lenses of its eyes can be

Astonishing fact

The males of seahorses, pipefishes, weedy and leafy sea dragons are the ones that get pregnant instead of the female of the species! This is unique and extreme in the animal world. When the time comes, the daddy gives birth to independent offspring!

Sea horse

seen. The eyes have a barrel shape and can be rotated to point either forward or straight up, looking through the fish's transparent dome.

The fish normally hangs nearly motionless in the water, at a depth of about 600 m to 800 m using its large fins for stability and with its eyes directed upward. It has been observed that when prey such as small fish and jellyfish are spotted, the eyes rotate like binoculars, facing forward as it turns its body from a horizontal to a vertical position to feed.

Pufferfish

The Pufferfish is very interesting type of fish which is also known as the blowfish, fugu, swellfish and globefish. When it is threatened, it puffs up to about twice its normal size by gulping water. Hence the name. There are about 100 species of pufferfish. Most pufferfish are found in the Atlantic, Pacific and Indian Oceans.

A remarkable feature of this fish is that many of its parts contain an extremely strong, paralyzing poison called tetrodoxin. This poison is about a thousand times deadlier than cyanide! There is no known antidote for this poison.

Pufferfish are carnivores or meat-eaters. They eat corals, sponges, sea urchins, other echinoderms, and small crustaceans.

Pufferfish when puffed up, are almost spherical. They range in size from just a few inches long to almost 2 ft. They have elastic skin.

Some interesting sea fish

Swordfish

The Swordfish, is a fish that has a long, sharp beak like mouth. It is a fast-swimming fish. They are found worldwide in all tropical, subtropical, and temperate seas. They live about 9 years.

Swordfish are carnivores or meat-eaters. They eat squid, octopus, fish, and crustaceans. Swordfish often kill their prey by swinging their sharp sword like bill from side to side within school of fish. A little later they eat the dead and wounded fish.

The biggest swordfish are about 14.5 ft long, and 540 kg in weight.

Astonishing fact
Seahorses are the only fish that swim upright.

Lanternfish

The lanternfish is an unusual, deep-sea fish with many light-producing organs in its body, especially in the belly. As the Lanternfish lives deep under the sea, it is very dark out there. It is then that its bio-luminescent organs light up the water as the fish swims. It uses its lights to attract its prey also.

Lanternfish have huge eyes and the largest Lanternfish are seldom over 1 ft long.

Lanternfish eat copepods which are small invertebrates with big eyes and long antennae and also amphipods like shrimps.

Astonishing fact
Sharks are the only fish which have eyelids!

Some interesting sea fish

Seahorses

Seahorses are a type of small fish that resemble horses. So, they are called seahorses. They have armored plates all over their body instead of scales that most fishes have. There are about 50 different species of seahorses around the world. They live in seaweed beds in warm water and they swim very slowly. Seahorses can change their colour to hide themselves from enemies. Among all the species, the Australian sea horse, which has leaf-like camouflage all over its body is the most unusual. It disappears in the seaweed bed due to its leafy body.

Seahorses vary in size from under a centimetre long to about 1 ft long. The female seahorse produces eggs, but they do not give birth. It is the male who gives birth about 40 to 50 days. The sea horse is the only animal in which the father is pregnant!

FISH

Sunfish

The **Ocean Sunfish** is said to be the heaviest of all bony fish in the world. The body of the **Ocean Sunfish** is very flat and its head and tail has a typical design. They can be 4.2 m long vertically and 3.1 m horizontally, weighing nearly 2,268 kg. They can range from gray to brown to silver in colour.

Sunfish tend to have darker colours on the top and lighter on the bottom. This helps them camouflage. Their bodies are covered with mucus rather than with scales.

Sunfish are found in temperate and tropical oceans around the world. Many a time the sunfish are seen basking in the sun near the surface and are often mistaken for sharks when they emerge out of water with their huge dorsal fins!

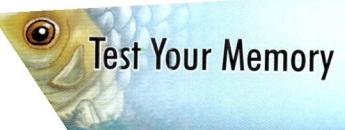

Test Your MEMORY

1. What are fish?

2. What is ichthyology and what are scientists who study fish called?

3. With the help of which organ do fish breathe?

4. What is the first vertebrate fossil that has been found?

5. When did vertebrates arise?

6. What does Agnatha mean?

7. Which is the most successful group of fish?

8. What are the three types of fishes according to anatomical structure?

9. What are the types of fishes according to salinity tolerance?

10. Why the Stonefish is called so?

11. What is the other name for Deep Sea Angler fish?

12. What is the name of light producing organ in fish?

FISH

Index

A

Agnatha 15
anadromous 18
aquarium 22

B

bioluminescence 13
bony fish 8, 16, 17
breathe 4, 6

C

cartilage 3, 15
cartilaginous 16
catadromous 18
cold-blooded 3
coldwater fish 17
counter shading 12

E

eggs 9
electric 14
eyes 9, 13, 25, 28

F

fins 4, 7, 8, 15, 17, 25
freshwater fish 17, 18

G

gills 4, 6, 16

J

jawless 15

L

lakes 3
lateral line 11
lungs 6

M

marine fish 13, 17, 23
migration 21

O

oceans 3, 21, 23, 26
omega 22
operculum 16

Osteichthyes 15, 16

P

protein 22
pupils 9

S

salinity 18, 20
salt 11, 17, 18, 20, 22
saltwater 18, 20, 22
scales 5, 15, 16, 29
species 4, 10, 13, 14, 17, 18, 19, 21, 22, 24, 25, 26, 29
swim bladder 10, 16

T

tropical fish 7, 17

V

venomous 23, 24
vertebrate 3, 28
vitamins 22